HOW TO GET COACHING CLIENTS

I would like to thank all those I have learnt from over the last few years that have enabled me to grow myself.

HOW TO GET COACHING CLIENTS

Are you on the More Client More Cash mailing list to keep up with the latest marketing tips specifically for the Personal Development industry?

Visit **www.moreclientmorecash.com** and pop your details on the form...

...hey there might just be a free special bonus for you. You will get to learn that I reward people who take action!

HOW TO GET COACHING CLIENTS

HOW TO GET COACHING CLIENTS

By

Jon Daniels

www.moreclientsmorecash.com

HOW TO GET COACHING CLIENTS

HOW TO GET COACHING CLIENTS

CONTENTS

SO HOW DO YOU ACTUALLY GET MORE COACHING CLIENTS? 9
WHY DO YOU WANT TO RUN YOUR OWN BUSINESS? 16
WHAT DO YOU ACTUALLY UNDERSTAND ABOUT YOUR CLIENTS?...... 26
JUST WHY SHOULD ANYONE LISTEN TO YOU? 34
HOW WILL YOU ACTUALLY MAKE MONEY BEING A COACH?............. 43
HOW WILL YOU ACTUALLY MAKE YOUR BUSINESS RUN?................... 51
WHAT ARE YOUR INCOME PRODUCING ACTIVITIES? 57
ARE YOU WALKING YOUR TALK? 67
SO WHAT IS YOUR BUSINESS PLAN? 77
BUSINESS DIAGNOSTIC Q&A 84

HOW TO GET COACHING CLIENTS

SO HOW DO YOU ACTUALLY GET MORE COACHING CLIENTS?

If you're sitting there at the moment, wondering where your next client's going to come from, and you're thinking, *How am I going to pay my bills next month*, you really need to sit comfortably and read on. So take the next couple of hours as a real investment into you, into your coaching business, of how you can turn things around to get more clients, to get more cash and make your coaching business a real success.

Before we begin, I'm just going to share this with you. I was one of those eighty percent of coaches that failed. I had to accept my life coaching business wasn't working. I had to face the embarrassment of all my friends and family that I had so proudly told that I was going to become a life coach that it wasn't working.

I had to go and get a full-time job again. And that really hurt. It really hurt my pride, particularly when I so believe in the power of coaching. It's an absolutely fantastic skill that I believe everyone should be able to use. Yet it hurt. It really hurt my pride when I didn't know how to sell it as a business, and I had to go back to full time work. I was still determined to be a success. I juggled two jobs as I vowed I would return as a successful coach.

Now the first thing I had to do was actually stop and realize I was listening to people who weren't actually that successful in coaching themselves. I stopped and I decided, *I'm going to listen to people who actually know what they're talking about*. Now, it took me another eighteen months before I got my first, actual paying coaching client. But in this time, two really interesting things happened.

HOW TO GET COACHING CLIENTS

Firstly, what had completely passed me by, in my full-time job; I was getting some really, really good deals on the table. I was negotiating multimillion pound contracts, with the likes of Halfords, the likes of Thornton's, First Group, Stagecoach and ICI; the list was endless. The list nearly passed me by, but I'd been learning all these new skills, and been applying them in a full-time job. I was so focused on my coaching business that I didn't actually notice how much of a difference it was making to me overall.

Now also, at the same time as this, my coaching business was becoming successful. I was getting another steady stream of paying customers and I was getting a good reputation. And, as you know, when you develop as a coach, you do build a nice little network of people that you graduated through your coaching course at the same time.

HOW TO GET COACHING CLIENTS

These people started coming to me, asking me, "How did you do it, Jon? How did you start getting all these clients?" And I noticed I was starting to coach them and show them how to do it themselves. So not only was I fixing my own business, I was also helping all my friends, who were coaches as well, turn their business around. And I thought, *Well, it's time to take this to another level. If I can do it for myself, and I can help other people, well, why not?*

That's what coaching is about. It's sharing the information and helping people become a success. I'm very passionate about helping people become successful coaches. But I also get the hardest thing to do is understand where you're going to get more clients and more cash from, so you can actually run a business. So I'm going to share with you the seven things that I've learned that you must do to get more clients and more cash.

HOW TO GET COACHING CLIENTS

Let's go right from the start. You've got to understand why you're setting up a business, let alone a coaching business—the commitment I had to make when I went back to full-time work to say, *No, I'm still going to run a successful coaching business*. I had reasons behind that, and you've got to establish them too. Why do you want to run your own business? Its hard work, and you need to understand that.

The other thing, as well, is that you need to start out understanding what your clients need. It's so easy to go, *I'm a life coach, and this is what my clients need*. But you need to ask yourself, Is that actually what they're asking for, or are you actually trying to give them what was a fabrication in your head, or it's an emotional attachment you have to an idea that you're very proud of. You need to work on that one.

The other thing you need to look at is why should anyone listen to you? No one cares how many letters you've got after your name. No one cares what certificates you've got. What people want to know is, why is this important to me, why do I need to know this? You need to get your head around it. It's not about you. It's about your customers, and you must, must be self-evident of why you are someone who must be listened to and what you're trying to sell.

The big thing is, you also need to understand—you must also have a strategy, and a strategy that you know will deliver cash into your business. You don't think people are just going to turn up there when you're sitting there doing nothing. You must understand what your strategy is of how you're actually going to make money.

You have to have the processes that support that strategy; that means when someone does pick up the phone and ring in, or if you do get a lead through a website, that you've got the ability to actually process them, to actually turn them into paying clients. You can't just sit back and wait for leads to come to you.

HOW TO GET COACHING CLIENTS

You have to be taking regular, consistent action out there.

And the big thing. The biggest thing. The biggest thing that really changed my whole business was, I had to walk my own talk as a coach. I had to start listening to the right people. I had to start being coached myself. And that's the biggest mistake I see people making in this industry.

Now this is a £15 billion industry. If you're not getting clients, it's got nothing to do with excuses. It's to do with you not offering the right value to the right people. So let's go into each of these seven reasons, just a little bit more, just so you can take away and start fixing your business right now, as these resonate with you, and you start to understand where your business is hurting you right now.

WHY DO YOU WANT TO RUN YOUR OWN BUSINESS?

Okay, so let's crack on with the first thing you must do if you want to attract more coaching clients.

Well, the first thing it's really key for you to do, is you must understand why you want to run your own business instead of doing a full-time job. Do you know if you have the business acumen and commercial awareness to run a business? Do you really get that? Just to get up and go, do you have the drive? Do you really understand why that's so important when running your own business? This isn't just about running a coaching business. This is about running any business that you've chosen to do.

Do you have the resolve to take things on the chin? Learn and drive yourself on? Do you enjoy the sales?

HOW TO GET COACHING CLIENTS

Do you enjoy the marketing? Do you enjoy customer service? Because you have to do it all. Are you able to pick up a set of accounts and understand what's going on? You need to get this business acumen if you're going to run your own business, because it's not the same as sitting there in a full-time job.

A full-time job, you get paid a nice salary for sitting there, for your time, nine to five each day—maybe more if you're doing overtime at the moment—but it's ridiculous to think it's the same when you're working for yourself, because it isn't. Your time is your money, and if you don't do any work, if you're off sick, you do not earn the money. It's as simple as that.

So, why do you want to run a coaching business? Is it just for some shits and giggles, because it seems like fun doing this, running your own business? You've been there, you've done all your training, you're thinking, *Hey, I'm a super life coach. I love it. I'm going to be brilliant.*

HOW TO GET COACHING CLIENTS

But really, you are genuinely having fun with all the learning, but you don't realize how serious it is when you actually take this to actually doing something for real. If you're doing it for the status, or thinking, *Yeah, I'm a life coach and I earn lots of money,* well, you are going to be in for a big, big shock, because it really isn't as easy as that when you're starting out.

Let me give you an idea of what it's actually like when you start in business. What it actually is like, is you become a wildebeest, where you're hunted daily. You're not hunted by clients. You're hunted by other businesspeople trying to get their hands into you. You need that new website. You need that new marketing course. You need the shit hot business cards. You need the shit hot flyers.

And you get caught up playing all these games, because everyone else is doing it. For example, I've seen so many people go, "Yeah, what's this Twitter?

HOW TO GET COACHING CLIENTS

I've got to be on Twitter." And they spend hours each day twittering away, but they don't even understand why they're doing it, because there's no strategy behind it. They're just doing it because everyone else is doing it, and they want to be seen with the cool kids, because that's what the rest of the pack do while hunting the wildebeest.

If you play these games with people, and not play your own game, you're just going to be sitting there worrying where your next client is coming from, you'll be worrying about paying the mortgage next month. You're soon going to have to face the embarrassment of all your friends and family, because you realise that you've got to go back to full-time work, because you were just having too much fun messing around, and really just masturbating away, enjoying yourself in the world of coaching. You didn't realise how serious it is if you're going to be a professional; and in fact, while you thought you were having fun wanking, you were actually masturbating with sandpaper, because that's the stress you've caused yourself.

You need to really understand why you don't want to work in a full-time job, why do you want to run your own business. And it can't be reasons such as I don't want to work nine to five; I don't want to be a slave to the man; I don't want to be a slave to the corporate world. Because they're all away from reasons for what you don't want.

And as you know as a coach, that's the worst thing that can happen if you're trying to do something to avoid something. You have to set your compelling reason of why you are running your own business. A half-assed reason you don't really care about really won't help you. Let's give you an example of what I mean by a compelling reason.

Imagine you were getting into a taxi, and when the driver turns around, he says, "Where to, boss?"

And you say, "Hmm. I don't know."

Well, that's great. You can't run your business that way, if you don't know where you're going. What about if you got in the taxi and the driver said, "Where don't you want to go?"

You go, "I don't want to go to Gatwick."

The driver's like, "Brilliant. Well, there's one place in the world you don't want to go."

You can't get motivated. You're not going anywhere by that. You need to pinpoint exactly where you're going. If you want to go to Heathrow, because you've got to catch a flight, you go, "Taxi driver, take me to Heathrow. Take me to the Departures Lounge, right outside that door, so I can get in, check out, and get there as quickly as possible."

That's what it's like when you're running a business. You have to have that compelling reason that acts like your body armor. It stops any games people are playing with you and try to put stuff on you. You have the certainty, you have the self-belief, and you are passionate about what you're doing. It doesn't matter if people try to distract you from your game. You are living your game. You're passionate about it, you care about it, and you do not need the approval of anyone else, because you have the certainty and belief in what you are doing.

You understand that it's your choice in what you're doing. You can always choose to do something. You can always choose to not do something. And you always have the choice to go, Hey, I don't even care, so I'm just going to walk away. You don't have to explain yourself. All you need to do is get yourself where you can make decisions, because it's going to help you get what you want to do. You have to focus on what you want, so you can go straight to completion.

You're not going to get caught up in other people's silly, little games, where it's distracting you from actually completing the tasks you want. You're not going to start taking on these tasks because you thought it would be a good idea. You're not actually finishing anything, because then you're just never going anywhere. You're just going to become more and more stressed and overwhelmed, with too much going on, and nothing delivering results.

So you need the belief. You need to be passionate. You need to give yourself self acceptance, right now, in what you're doing. You will understand you have choice, you will understand you make the decisions, and you complete whatever you set out to do, because it's your business, no one else's. And this is so important in running your own business, these compelling reasons to give you the drive, because it's

HOW TO GET COACHING CLIENTS

like putting the solid foundation blocks in place for what you're doing.

Think about it in the Bible. There's the man who built his house on sand, and there's the man who built his house on rock. Which one survived? The person who put the solid foundations in. If you build your house on sand, it's going to come crashing down at the first sight of a big storm that comes near you.

What you want to be is, think of a big iceberg, that when a big ship comes up into the sea, that there's so much underneath the water you can't see, nothing is going to knock that bad boy out of the way. Anyone, even if he's a giant, that's a Goliath and you're little David, is still going to bring that big boy down, because you know what you're doing, and you are passionate about it.

Just think when you're building a tall skyscraper. Do you start putting the seats in the roof, or do you start on the top floor in the ceiling, or do you start really far, down underground, putting in those solid, concrete blocks that just make you so completely stable.

I cannot express enough, the first thing you need to do; to get more clients is get your compelling reason why you want to run your own coaching business.

WHAT DO YOU ACTUALLY UNDERSTAND ABOUT YOUR CLIENTS?

So the next stop, we need to start looking at how you actually understand what your customers want. I need to get you aligned with what your customers actually need. See, I've got some big news for you. If you haven't figured it out already, the life coaching ship has already set sail. You have missed the boat if you're still marketing yourself as a generalist life coach.

Your clients will be much more attracted to you if you fulfill a specific need for them. The days of the generalist life coach are well and truly over. And I will bet you, if you know someone who's actually doing well as a life coach, it's because they've been doing it for a long time. No one, in the last couple of years, has broken through as a generalist life coach because the market is gone. It's saturated with coaches. It's being a specialist and understanding specific needs of your customers.

This really came home to me when I was listening to an interview with James Lavers and Alex Smith, who some of you may well know as Jonathan Royle. What Alex actually said in that interview was, "You cannot be something to everyone. You have to be something to someone."

The fact is, you cannot please everyone all of the time, and you've got to get that into your head. If you're being a generalist life coach, you're trying to please everyone, and you just can't do it. But what you can do is be the specialist, be the expert, and you can do something very specific to please someone.

Too many coaches today are resisting finding a niche, and if you're one of these coaches, you're going to be the one sitting there, worrying about where your next client's coming from. You're going to be worrying about paying the rent next month, and you're not going to be in business in twelve months' time. It's as simple as that.

What you really need to accept, is you won't lose customers by actually being a specialist. It's a powerful, powerful paradox, but the more narrow your niche, the more narrow you pick a market, the more clients you actually get, because you'll be seen as an expert.

Let me take this a little bit further. Let's take a pair of socks. How do you sell a pair of socks? Go on, just answer that in your head. You've got a pair of socks. How do you sell them?

Well, how about if I was to give you a pair of pink, fluffy socks, and ask you to sell them to an eight-year-old girl? What about if I gave you a verruca sock, to ask you to sell it to someone with a verruca? How about if I gave you a pair of silk socks, with diamond-encrusted tops, and asked you to sell them to a chief executive?

What happens when just doing that very, very simple exercise, just looking at socks? Wasn't it easier when I gave you a specific person to sell a specific item to? See, the prospect of selling to a narrow audience is actually better because it becomes easier, because it makes more sense of who you're actually trying to communicate with.

So, you can really start seeing the importance of niching. But this market moves so fast, and by the way, change is the only constant you'll find when you're running a business. You must be flexible, and I recommend you read a book called *Who Moved My Cheese*, by Spencer Johnson, because that's all about adapting to change.

But back on the point. Niching was the hot word in the last eighteen months, but it's not really niching, now. It's moved on again. What you're actually looking at is fulfilling needs. You need to actually step into your customer's skin, walk a mile in their shoes. You need to live and breathe to understand what's going on.

You need to understand the pain they're in, in their everyday life. You need to understand the urgency in their everyday life, with what they're going through— the pain, the urgency—and you need to speak to these people. You need to find out exactly what they're looking for, because then you can give them exactly what they need. And that's what you'll be a specialist in. You'll be the expert in that field of fulfilling that need.

And the moment I did this in my business—and I'm talking within hours, I kid you not—I started making money. And let me just walk you through this, as an example.

You might have heard of this as superniching, by the likes of Dan Bradbury, who's teaching this. But it's not superniching. It's identifying a need in people that will give you your clients. So let's take an example.

I started out as a generalist life coach, and I realised I needed a niche, so I chose confidence. And I started doing a little bit better, but not brilliantly. But what I then did, is I really looked at, what is it about confidence? Because you see, confidence is a really broad subject. You can have shyness about speaking in meetings, you can have blushing when talking to people, you can have dating shyness or you can have issues about not being confident because you're trying to avoid conflict.

What I noticed, that everyone who I was speaking to—the people I was gathering on my list—the feedback was they were sick and tired of being knocked over constantly by people and being walked all over. So that became my niche. I became the go-to guy for people who felt they were constantly being knocked down and walked all over by people. And the moment that I just focused on that market, and started speaking to those people, I started making more money, because these were the people that started resonating with what I was saying. It was as simple as that.

Let's take another niche. For example, there are a lot of people who do stop smoking coaching. Well, the moment I changed it to stop smoking in Oxford, and stop smoking for soon-to-be mothers, stop smoking for grandparents, stop smoking for people that doctors have given up on—as soon as I started identifying these superniches with different needs, and really resonated with these needs, my business started growing. I started getting more clients. I started getting more cash.

HOW TO GET COACHING CLIENTS

And when you adopt this philosophy, the possibilities become endless. The more specific you can be, the more needs that you can fulfill with your service, the more clients you will get, because you're more in touch with them, they really resonate with you, and you will be more successful. Fact.

JUST WHY SHOULD ANYONE LISTEN TO YOU?

I bet now you've done some research, that you're actually feeling a lot better about yourself, because you can really see how your sales can be made so much easier to get more coaching clients. But now you've done your research. It's all about the delivery. You need to now work out why anyone should listen to you.

If you honestly think people are going to come up and welcome you into their life, and want to know all about what you do in your services, think again, because it really doesn't work like that. In reality, it's more like, I don't know you, I don't like you and I know you're going to bloody try to sell me something as well, aren't you?

HOW TO GET COACHING CLIENTS

So let me throw this back at you. Imagine being interviewed on TV by someone like Richard Madeley. He doesn't care about how many letters you've got after your name. He doesn't care how many certificates you've got. He just wants to find out why anyone should be interested in listening to you, and he will grill you to make sure you're worth speaking to. He'll need to make sure your message is something that the world needs to hear.

You have to stop massaging your own ego. Stop the ego wanking. Stop the fabrications. Stop the disillusions you have going on in your head. You must demonstrate what you can do for your clients. Quite simply, you must know how to passionately, and with certainty, answer the question, why should anyone listen to you?

People will make assumptions about you before you've even met them. They will just think, "Oh, shit, not another bloody life coach." And these people normally have good reasons to think about coaching in this way. It all comes down to a word called congruence.

Picture this. Imagine there's a fat weight loss coach. How about a stop smoking coach who smokes sixty a day? How about a divorced and lonely woman who does relationship coaching? How about a struggling business coach with no clients? Or what about a confidence coach who fears public speaking? One more. How about a life coach suffering a midlife crisis?

Well, I can relate to that, because that was me. I knew when I was in an NLP course, because I was in the middle of a full-blimied life crisis. I had quit my job after calling my boss the c-word and threatened to punch him. I shaved all my hair off. Ended a six-year relationship. And to make it all make sense, I went and trained with Paul McKenna to become a hypnotist.

HOW TO GET COACHING CLIENTS

Well, there's some logic for you. Probably not the most ideal way to start a business, and not surprisingly, I ended up back in full-time employment, within a year, as I mentioned earlier, because I didn't have any clients and didn't really have any business sense.

I had to face the embarrassment of all my friends and family, to tell them that in my big dream, that I quit my high-flying job, for what was all basically just me ego-wanking, trying to massage my own ego and to make out I was Mr. Big, thinking, Yeah, I'm a life coach, and I'm going to earn lots of money. And in all reality, I didn't have a clue what I was doing. In fact, I didn't know what I was doing with my life over all.

One thing I did get out of it was, though, people did like me. The problem was, no one understood what the hell I was actually offering. In fact, I didn't know what I was actually offering, myself. I was having a lot of fun, but I wasn't really making any money. And trust me, the fun stops the moment you realise you can't pay the mortgage next month, and you can't face your friends and family without lying to them about how well things are going.

It wasn't until I did a course with a couple of NLP trainers and you might know them—Nick Kemp and Tina Taylor. And they did this exercise that really got the point to click with me, of why should anyone listen to me? I was on a presentation course in Leeds, and I did this storytelling with emotions exercise.

Now, I mentioned earlier about the shift I made from just being a coach to being a confidence coach, to helping people who are constantly getting knocked down by other people. Well during this exercise, I was telling everyone stories that made it self-evident I was some sort of expert on the subject of being knocked down and walked all over by other people.

HOW TO GET COACHING CLIENTS

What this really proved to me was that if you can communicate passionately about the needs that you fulfill for your clients, and you can be self-evident in this, then you have earned the right to be an authority on this subject. And because of your life experiences, people will see you as the go-to person for that particular need.

This is what congruence is. You are fulfilling the need that matches how you speak, how you sound, how you look. People can really resonate with you, and hold you as the expert on the matter that they're interested in, because you're walking your own talk.

I can look at where I am, right now. I've told you. I've already set up a coaching business. So why am I doing marketing for coaches? Well firstly, as I said, I've walked my own talk. I created a successful coaching business. I'm one of the twenty percent who made it. I was one of the eighty percent that had to go back to work. I kept going. I believed in myself, and I made it.

HOW TO GET COACHING CLIENTS

Everything I am telling you in this book is a personal, firsthand learning experience, that took me from worrying where my next client was going to come from, to having a room full of people that were always ready to listen to me, give me feedback, and really enjoy what I was sharing with them.

Secondly, this also made me notice that I had a lot of issues around confidence when I was younger and growing up, and it's what led to my midlife crisis, because I had reached that point of enough was enough.

But aside from that, over the last ten years, I had a very, very successful career. I've been in sales for the last ten years, and like coaching, I was selling a service, and something that's intangible. By that, I mean, something you can't pick up, something you can't touch. You just can't pick this up and put it in a wheelbarrow. You can't stroke it like a pet. It's not something you can walk into a shop and pull it off the shelf.

These are what services are, and I've been selling these to an award-winning level, selling multimillion pound contracts for ten years. And this made me realise that, again, I can be congruent as a marketing coach because I've walked my own talk in coaching. I've shown you can build successful businesses.

But I've been selling services for years, and I've been bloody good at it. And because people had already started coming to me, asking for a little help in setting up their coaching businesses, this for me shows that I'm congruent and it showed I've already earned a degree of status in what I'm doing. It's now time to make it grow, because I tested what I'm doing. I believe in it, and now people have to listen to me, because I've earned the right to talk to them. I've earned the right to be an authority.

HOW TO GET COACHING CLIENTS

The secret to this, the secret to selling an intangible service, is to help your customers go from, "I don't know you. I don't like you," to meeting you, knowing you, liking you and then trusting you, so you earned the right to fulfill their needs for them.

In this industry, you really do reap what you sow. Congruence is absolutely key in running a coaching business. And just as a final thought here, imagine you were going to go onto a program like Dragons' Den. What is the passionate, self-evident message that you would give to a dragon that shows that you have 100 percent belief in what you are doing? Why should a dragon listen to you?

HOW WILL YOU ACTUALLY MAKE MONEY BEING A COACH?

Now once you've finished your coaching training, I totally get that no one actually tells you how to make any real money in the coaching business. Coaching schools are great at training and selling training. They're not so good at teaching how to run a coaching business.

I'll also tell you that most coaches cannot stand the thought of selling. I know people who are scared to answer the phone, let alone ask for an order, or to actually state confidently and with conviction the amount for their services. So I have an approach that I think you will like. I call it the no selling approach to selling.

HOW TO GET COACHING CLIENTS

I mentioned earlier that I've been in a sales team for over ten years. The reason this wasn't actually apparent to me was because I never actually saw myself as a salesman. I just thought I was good at talking to people. I was good at listening to what people needed, then giving them a solution that made them happy for what they wanted.

That's influence in a nutshell, for you, by the way. The big secret to selling is to actually just watch and listen, as people will tell you everything you need right away. You just need to understand where they're coming from and then match what you have to offer to their reality.

In fact, I think the only reason I won a multimillion pound contact from the likes of Halfords, once, was because I showed the decision maker of the company how to play Mario Kart in exhibition. I built a relationship with him that went beyond just talking shop. He got to know me, like me, and trust me, and

HOW TO GET COACHING CLIENTS

then realised I was the man for the job. I don't think we were necessarily the biggest or the cheapest provider out there, that's for sure.

Your customers have a context that their world is built around. Whatever you offer must reference to their world. For example, people who lack confidence cannot reference being confident, as it just scares them. It pushes them too far into the unknown too quickly. If you talk to them about not being knocked down and walked all over, they can totally relate to it, because they have the experience to reference against it. The more clearly you can define your clients, the more you will get.

For example, I got a referral once from someone I met, about two months earlier, just in passing. He knew me as the guy who helps people out who are being bullied. The moment he met someone being bullied, he immediately and proudly referred me to them. Did I need to sell to those people? Absolutely not, as someone they trusted told them about me. People buy people, and your product is coaching. The more you can make your intangible service real, like a product, like something people can pick up and feel, the easier it is for the customer to understand and buy into the idea.

You need to build a crowd around you to see you as the expert in that area. Find out what they want, not what you think they want, then give it to them. People hate being sold to, but they love to buy. You build the relationship with them. When you offer something, they will buy it without you needing to pitch it and hard-sell.

So here are the basics of how you get cash into your coaching business. There are three ways you can grow your business. One is to increase the number of orders, two is to put the prices up, and three is to increase the amount of times current customers buy with you.

HOW TO GET COACHING CLIENTS

Getting the first sale, at the right price is the toughest work you'll ever have to do. Once someone has bought once, and totally gets the value from you, they become a fan and continue to buy more. This means the bulk of your costs are in acquiring customers, as it's converting them into leads, into sales in the first place, and then getting them into the sales funnel.

So what is a sales funnel, I hear you ask. Well, here's an easy way for you to create your funnel. Your funnel has three levels. Anything you create at the top of the funnel must provide *what to do* information. These are the quick tips that are fast acting pain relief like Nurofen, like when you have a headache and you want to get rid of it. This is the free information you give away.

I don't mean another newsletter saying the same old crap everyone else is saying. Come up with something cool, that's totally different, totally shows your offer, the self-evident expert who gets your clients. Your free stuff should be like fast-acting pain relief. This information should work so well, it just leaves your clients wanting more and more. That's when they move down the funnel to your medium-level prices. This is the how-to knowledge, where you need to give away a bit more of the game.

So for example, in my free report for MoreClientsMoreCash.com, I told you what was needed was a cash-making strategy for your coaching business. I then offer audio classes as one of my medium products, where I'm telling you how to get a cash-making strategy.

By this time, your clients will be getting the value of what you offer and be willing to pay you more for your personal one-to-one time at the higher price at the end of your funnel.

Your funnel is all about meet, like, know, trust and then doing business together. As long as you keep stacking value, people will buy from you. And just remember to leverage your time using products, to get people to trust you without charging you for your time.

If you charge low prices for your time, you really don't have anywhere else to go, and won't make the money in your coaching business that you actually want to make. You must avoid ego-wanking about what you think people want. Find out what they actually want first, then give it to them. Don't get emotionally tied to your ideas. Go with what people actually want.

People ask me how much should they charge for their coaching services. The answer really is, how long is a piece of string? Different markets have different caps on what you can charge. But ultimately, it's down to what you feel comfortable charging, against the value you show your leads. As I said at the start, it's about

HOW TO GET COACHING CLIENTS

you, telling your prices with confidence and conviction.

Jairek Robbins, Tony Robbins' son, came up with a really cool way to sort your pricing out. Just charge something to start with, that you're so comfortable with, that people will buy. If that means starting it free, that's fine. Then every time you make five sales at that level, put your prices up a bit, and sell five more, and so on and so on. The only cap is you holding yourself back. Just have fun, and just really, really go for it.

HOW WILL YOU ACTUALLY MAKE YOUR BUSINESS RUN?

So now you know what a funnel is, you can build one. But what you also need is a process to guide them, from prospect to lead, to customer, to high-priced coaching client. Each step you need to keep adding value and building the trust.

The first step is to build a crowd. I'll come back to lead generation strategies later, but for now, let's look at turning a prospect into a lead. How do you get someone who finds you to give you their contact details so you can start to build a relationship with them?

So first things first. Someone finds you. How do they know that they are in the right place? Is it your business card? Is it your Web site? Have they just heard your elevator pitch? How do they know who you are and what you do?

You have about four seconds on first impression to get someone's attention, so how are you going to stand out by being unique and eye-catching? As a concept, think about this. If you just walk up to someone, straightway in a room, and go, "Hi, buy this expensive coaching package from me." If someone did that to you, are you likely to buy from them, being this forward and blunt, like with a direct salesman. Well, no one is going to buy that. No one likes that. I don't think you would, either.

But what if you were crystal clear in what you offer, and are giving away something for free, as a big, fat bribe. That big, fat bribe is like a magnet to someone who needs your services. In exchange for their contact details, they can have this big, fat free bribe. And remember, this bribe needs to be your most powerful, fast-acting pain relief technique that will make your new lead stand up and take notice.

I will start here for you. On average, it takes five to seven interactions with someone to go through the meet, know, like, trust process in order to buy from you. So what you now need to do is follow-up with them. You've met them, but what are three more fast-acting pain relief techniques you can offer them, straightaway, to build the relationship? How can they get to know you more intimately? How can they get to like you and how can they get to trust you?

On the trust touch point, it's important to tell your lead one more thing, as well. You need to tell them how much you are enjoying sharing this information with them, and will have something to offer them, next time you contact them. If you have gone through the meet, know, like, trust model correctly, the trust is there, and it's important you come clean and tell them you're about to make them an offer.

HOW TO GET COACHING CLIENTS

You don't want it to come as a surprise, and put them on the spot, so they feel uncomfortable. If they've liked everything you shared with them so far, their human nature will allow you the opportunity to make them your offer, and in all honesty, it will be the shortest sales pitch you have ever made, because by this point, you'll be just showing them what's on offer and what you'll send them or what you'll do for them. They will have already made their mind up by this point, if they ever want to work with you.

Bear in mind, the people who won't want to work with you will have dropped out long before this point, so you'll be making your offer to a bona fide, qualified, interested lead. This is a technique I've tried and tested so many times, and it's something you can put on autopilot. This shit really works, trust me.

Now a key point I touched on here is leveraging your time. Imagine your hourly rate is £100. For every hour you spend doing admin and processing tasks, that's £100 lost on coaching fees for your time. Your processes need to be as automated as possible, so you can spend more time on growing your business and more time doing paid appointments instead of doing admin and processing tasks.

Leveraging your time doesn't mean having too much fun avoiding actually trying to do any work, whatsoever, because you don't know how to get clients, you don't know how you're going to pay the mortgage next month, and in reality, you're just facing the embarrassment of seeing all your friends and family and going back to work. You really must learn how to put a process behind your cash making strategy that's going to make life as easy for you as possible.

HOW TO GET COACHING CLIENTS

HOW TO GET COACHING CLIENTS

WHAT ARE YOUR INCOME PRODUCING ACTIVITIES?

Let's have a quick recap, because I know I've downloaded a lot on you so far.

You now know about identifying your customer's needs. You know about creating a sales funnel, and you know about implementing a simple sales strategy. So theoretically, what you now have is a room with a stage. It's your stage, and the room is clearly marked so people know exactly what to expect if they go into that room.

Once in the room, it's like a selling machine, as your funnel shows people exactly what to do. I know, this room sounds like magic. The problem is, you can spend months thinking about it. You can spend months putting this process together, and you can spend months aggressively waiting for the phone to ring, and tell them about your magic room. But unless people know about your room, no one is going to be in it, and it doesn't matter how good the room is—if no one is in it, it's not worth anything, and you're not in business. You're only in business when you're providing the value to your clients, and they recognise it.

It's like money. If I gave you a £10 note, and you just hung onto it, it isn't actually worth anything; in fact, the longer you hold onto it, its worth less and less. So if you do decide to spend it, it's not worth what it was in the first place. Money only has a value when you spend it in that moment, and it's like the information in this book. It's worthless unless you use it.

The big lesson to learn here is, all the other steps are vital to planning your business, but each of those steps are really fluid. You must be flexible or willing to change as you learn. You need to get into the mentality of having fun, experimenting and learning along the way. You've got to step up and take action. Instead of thinking about what could be, you need to just go and do it, and learn.

Once you have the skill to create the moneymaking magic room that runs on autopilot, you can put all your effort and all your focus on just filling the room. You'll not fill the room, as I said, by aggressively waiting for the phone to ring. What you need to do, and in the words of the great Brad Burton is, "Get off your ass, and tell people about you."

I heard this interview with a guy called Mark Layder recently. Mark was doing coaching in NLP, long before it even was recognized as a concept in this country; before they even had a name of coaching in NLP. This is how long this guy's been doing it.

He stated two things that are really important to get the sales in. Firstly, it's to set up a base camp, either

HOW TO GET COACHING CLIENTS

at home or in your office, but somewhere where you can work, uninterrupted each day, for whatever amount of time you set.

Secondly, he says you need to focus on your income-producing activity each day. If you do an hour a day, you're likely to earn in the region of £20,000 a year. If you do three hours a day, you will earn a triple-figure income.

So what are your income-producing activities? These are the activities that get your prospects to take a specific action. It's the action of accepting a big, fat bribe and turning it into a qualified lead that you can build a relationship with at the start of your funnel.

Your income-producing activities are where you announce to the world who you are, what needs you fulfill, and why you are the self-evident expert. And you can back it all up by offering risk-free pain relief to back up your big, bold claims.

I got to watch a talk with Barry Gibbons once. He used to be the CEO of Burger King. He tells the story of how he first went into Burger King, and he just felt it was ho hum. Same old shit as everywhere else was offering. And he went on about how he changed the Burger King image from ho fucking hum to offering something completely different, that gave them a unique experience when anyone went into a Burger King restaurant.

And that's what you need to do. You need to get out there, be bold, telling people about what you do. No ho fucking hum rubbish. Tell them about the research you have done. Look at your life stories in delivering something unique, so people clearly get what you do. And it's this message, it's this passion, it's this belief that must be the blood of every income producing activity that you do.

HOW TO GET COACHING CLIENTS

I could sit here and tell you twenty-odd income-producing activities, or lead generation strategies—whatever you want to call them right now—but they have all personally worked for me. They've gone from someone who didn't know me, taken them right through to the sales stage.

There are probably hundreds of tried and tested ways out there. They'll probably give you hundreds more in the next generation of entrepreneurs that we'll come up with. It's down to you to choose what's right for your business. It's what serves you to give you the congruent image that we've talked about before.

You have old school, offline activities, such as networking, canvassing, referrals and direct mail. All of them, as you know, you don't just walk straight up to them and go, "All right mate, can I have a sale off you?" You know you've got to build trust in what you're doing.

HOW TO GET COACHING CLIENTS

But you also have these new, online methods. Today's technology is outstanding, how quickly you can be connected to people all over the world. I couldn't believe it in my coaching business, that one call I had someone in India, someone in Australia, someone in Sweden and someone in America. It's just unbelievable. At one point, I got really popular in South Africa as well, and I've made some great contacts down there. But see, you've got all these great online methods that are so easy to use, like Google AdWords, if you get that right.

Old school writing. You can immediately be a published author who's seen as an expert. You've got YouTube now. YouTube is so easy to do. You can get a little Flip camcorder, record yourself for thirty seconds. YouTube's developed so much that people respond to conferencing videos now. You can be watching X Factor and people do live critiques, there and then. It's absolutely amazing. The possibilities are endless.

But what you must decide on is the five or so activities that you're going to do, consistently each day, to get people into your magic room to hear what you have to say. You're looking for them to take a specific course of action, which is, of course, to accept your big, fat bribe in exchange for contact details so you can continue to build the relationship with them; so you can continue to get back to that point of I don't know you, I don't like you all the way through to, I've met you, I like you, I trust you, and now I'm going to do business with you.

So don't sit on your arse aggressively waiting for the phone to ring. Worrying about where your next client is going to come from is certainly going to be worrying about paying the mortgage next month. Get off your bum and start telling the world about your big, fat bribe.

HOW TO GET COACHING CLIENTS

So when someone finds you, show them they're in the right place for their needs. Give them exactly what they are looking for, and make it easy for them; even better off than when they first heard of you. Show them that you're authentic. Show them that you understand how they feel, and let them think they've discovered a wonderful secret by finding you. Tell them exactly what to do next, and just eliminate any risk for them. Your income-producing activities are the blood flow of your business.

HOW TO GET COACHING CLIENTS

HOW TO GET COACHING CLIENTS

ARE YOU WALKING YOUR TALK?

So what is the seventh and final thing you must do to get more coaching clients? Well, this one for me is really key. I think it's something you will relate to. It's all about walking your talk.

I've already mentioned about being self-evident, that you're the expert in your niche. Now I will say this in plain English for you: nothing screams incongruency more than a relationship guru who's repeatedly in and out of dysfunctional relationships, a wealth trainer who's consistently broke, a health expert who's frequently sick due to a poor diet and an unhealthy lifestyle, and a coach whose life is in an absolute mess.

Now listen. I'm not saying you need to be perfect. God knows I'm not, and I'm not saying that you need to be better than your clients, either. But whatever you are coaching on, you do not need to be better than them. But as Mahatma Gandhi said, "You must be the change you wish to see in the world."

This is how to start getting more coaching clients and more cash in your business. In this book, I'm literally giving you the answers to getting more clients, right now, in today's economy.

When starting out, I had such low confidence in my business ability, that I failed to see that I wasn't valuing myself, and I was also preventing my clients from seeing the value, by not being congruent, and asking them for what I was actually worth. So many coaches suffer from this terrible mistake, that no only do they stay poor, but there's a far bigger issue. Their selfishness prevents them from truly giving the gift to people, and as many people as they possibly can out there.

HOW TO GET COACHING CLIENTS

One of the best things you can do to attract clients to you, is to get your own life in order, or at the very least, start setting some goals, and actually move towards getting your life sorted. Just make the effort. If you are the personification of the changes that the client most needs, they will feel compelled to do business with you, and this is the key to being flooded with more clients than you can handle.

For example, don't think it's realistic for me to go out there and say, "I'm the go-to guy if you want to be thin," because clearly, I need to drop a bit of weight, myself. However, I am in a position to say, "I can make you quit smoking." Why? Because I used to be a forty-a-day man myself, and I've helped many people give up since. I know the three key mindset changes that are needed to give up smoking forever.

I'm in a position to help people who have been bullied, who are constantly being knocked down, and are always being walked over by other people. Why is

HOW TO GET COACHING CLIENTS

that? Because I've been there myself, and I know what you must do to turn things around. And I totally get the frustrations of being in this situation.

I know how to get more coaching clients. I've done it for myself. I've done it for other people, and I will continue to do so. I have walked my own talk to be an expert in my chosen niche.

However, this is not the only walk I must make. There's another key part to this, and this is where I see coaches messing up all the time. You are a coach, you understand the value of coaching, so why don't you bloody have a coach yourself, then? It's okay. I forgive you. It would be hypocritical of me not to do so, as I didn't have a coach for a year, myself, after qualifying.

But for crying out loud, just go and get yourself a coach, a mentor, even a MasterMind group. Actually, preferably, get all three. Honestly, how can you expect to sell your coaching if you don't, 100 percent, in your heart of hearts, believe in it yourself?

Listen. When I had no clients and no money coming in, I still found ways to invest in myself. I read books. I listened to CDs. I attended seminars, and so on. Even when everyone around me told me to give up and get a regular job—in fact, especially when everyone told me to give up and get a regular job—I stuck to it.

You either believe in this stuff, or you don't. You either live this stuff or you don't. But either way, it will come across unconsciously to your potential clients, in every single action you take, because they are judging you. The question is, how do you measure up for what they're looking for?

If you're going to make a successful career selling your advice, or otherwise coaching people, you need to face the plain and simple fact that all people make instant, unconscious judgments about you, based on

HOW TO GET COACHING CLIENTS

what you look and sound like. Whether it is justified or not, you are, and will continue to be judged, based upon what a potential client sees or hears within seconds of meeting you. You must walk your own talk, and be the shining example for what your client needs. And you cannot do this by sitting on your bum, not continuing to learn for yourself.

So ask yourself. Who is your coach? Who is your mentor? Who do you follow and learn from? What books are you reading that help you develop?

Running a business is lonely, so having that coach, that mentor, that MasterMind group, really helps you massively, if you're looking at working on an idea or overcoming your obstacles.

At first, I just sat there, not telling anyone I was struggling. I did the British thing of keeping a stiff upper lip, when in public, that everything was okay. I kept my pride in tact.

I've opened up a bit to my good friends Vince and Val Knight, who I met during my NLP training. These guys have trained for so many hours with the experts, that running an idea by them are almost as good speaking directly to the likes of a Richard Bandler or Michael Neill. I have my own little MasterMind group right in front of me.

And guess what? When we started talking about these things, all of a sudden results started to improve. I continued. I trained with the likes of Chris Howard, Tony Robbins, Eric Edmonds, Frank Furness, John LaValle. I was like this seminar junkie for about eighteen months.

Then I started looking at confidence and self-esteem experts, and trained with the likes of Dawn Breslin, Pam Linford, David DeAngelo, Hypnotica, Alistair Horscroft—all these people who knew about confidence and self-esteem and lifestyle design. And everything I learned, I filtered into my type need that I was filling for my clients. I was filtering my learning, so that whatever these guys said, it could become relevant to my market and to the needs of my clients.

As I went through all the confidence and the smoking things, I then learned, as I said, I was helping a lot of people grow their businesses. So I started to learn more about the marketing, and I discovered the likes of James Lavers, Paul Avins, Evan Pagan, Dan Bradbury. The list goes on. You've got Mark Layder, Nick James—each one of these people contributing their own nuggets of gold I found for growing my own business.

At one point it hit home to me, so much, that I didn't have a coach, that I said on the next offer from a particular person, I was going to sign up, regardless of price, just to prove the value of coaching.

HOW TO GET COACHING CLIENTS

Well, it's not cheap. I got more out of that coaching relationship that anything else I've previously done. You have to walk your own talk. You have to be congruent. And as a coach, you must believe in coaching. So use coaching in your own development. Walk your own talk.

SO WHAT IS YOUR BUSINESS PLAN?

So that's it for this book. That's the seven reasons why you're not getting enough coaching clients. I've given you seven things you must do to start getting coaching clients. These are the very same ideas, concepts, and tips that took me from sitting there worrying where my next client was coming from and worrying about paying the mortgage, to having a flood of clients, and a roomful of people that were always interested to hear what I had going on.

Just to recap. If you're not getting enough clients and you're not getting enough cash into your business, your coaching business will fail, and that's a fact. And the good news is that we've gone through the seven reasons that are causing you to not get enough clients.

HOW TO GET COACHING CLIENTS

There's you don't actually know why you set up a coaching business. You have no understanding of what your ideal clients actually need. You cannot demonstrate why anyone should listen to you. You don't have a strategy that will bring cash into your business. You don't have any processes that will support your plan. You just aggressively sit back and wait for the phone to ring, and you don't walk your own talk.

The good news is, now that you know these seven reasons, you can save yourself a lot of unnecessary pain and wasting time by working out where your business is hurting you right now, and going and fixing the problem.

You now know you need your compelling reasons of why you want to set up a coaching business. You now know you need to go and do the research and really work out what your ideal client actually needs. You need to step into their skin, walk a mile in their shoes, be them, see the world through their eyes.

You need to look at your own personal experiences, and tell people why they should listen to you. Make it self-evident that you are an expert; you are an authority in what you're talking about.

Have a look at your sales funnel, and make sure you've got strategy there to actually bring clients into your business, because if you've got the clients, you've got the cash coming in. Then you are actually in business, and not just having fun ego-wanking about being a life coach.

You've got to have the process in there that allows you to leave with your time, as much as possible, to your either being paid for doing income-producing activity, or you're actually being paid for doing appointments, and that's the high-end appointments that's worth your money.

HOW TO GET COACHING CLIENTS

Don't sit back and aggressively wait for the phone to ring. Pick five or so things where you can do your income-producing activity consistently every day, so it works for you.

And finally, and the big thing, walk your own talk. If you want to be a successful life coach, invest in coaching. Live the life of a coach, and be a coach. If you have coaching, as a coach, you're only going to get better and better. Trust me.

So we've gone through loads and loads in the last fifty minutes or so. And what I'm going to do, is I'm going to give you the quickest business plan you'll ever need now, and ask you nine questions. The quicker you can answer these nine questions, by going through what I've talked about on this disk, the more clients, the more cash you're going to have in your business. I do not want you sitting there, worrying about where you next client's going to come from, and I certainly don't

HOW TO GET COACHING CLIENTS

want you worrying about paying your mortgage or your rent next month.

> **YOUR BUSINESS PLAN**
>
> 1. Who Is Your Target Market?
>
> 2. Who Is The Person & What Pain Are They In?
>
> 3. How Can You Find Out Exactly What They Need?
>
> 4. Why Are You Different To Anyone Else?
>
> 5. What Are The Steps In Your Sales Funnel?
>
> 6. What Five Ways Will You Generate Leads?
>
> 7. What Five Things Must You Measure?

HOW TO GET COACHING CLIENTS

> 8. Where Are You Bleeding Right Now?
>
> 9. What Is Your Compelling Reason?

Now I guarantee you, when you do this, and you can answer those questions, the whole world is going to open up to you, with opportunities, and instead of sitting there worrying where your clients are coming from, you're going to be like a magnet, attracting the people to you, because you are self-evident and clear on what services you offer and the needs you fulfill.

But it wouldn't be right, before I sign off, if I didn't make you my own big, fat bribe. So here it is.

I reward people who take action. And if you've got this far in this book, that means you're someone who does take action, and you're someone who is prepared to listen and invest in the effort and in yourself. So as I said, I'm going to reward you with that.

All you need to do is go to...

www.moreclientsmorecash.com/bigfatbribe.html

HOW TO GET COACHING CLIENTS

BUSINESS DIAGNOSTIC Q&A

Question: *I always thought I wanted to run a business to earn lots of money but this does not leave me feeling compelled as you describe. Why is this?*

My Comments: Money will never provide you with a compelling reason to do something as it only has value when you spend it. If you don't know what you actually want to buy or the lifestyle you want to fund, the amount of money is meaningless. You could say you want to earn one million pounds a year but in fact the life you actually want to live can easily be achieved by earning fifty thousand pounds a year.

The reality of achieving an income of fifty thousand pounds is a lot more comprehendible that one million pounds but without working that out your brain cannot actually function correctly. Your brain must be able to reference what you want to achieve.

HOW TO GET COACHING CLIENTS

Money will not motivate you in the long term. You must work out exactly what you want and then go for it until you have it. And I mean exactly what you want. If you want an £800 jacket, you keep going until you get that exact £800 jacket and not the £100 rip of version you can find down the market. You are just undervaluing yourself by taking the cheaper option and this message will be received by your subconscious. Go for what you are worth.

So instead of focusing on how much money you want to earn, look at what you actually want to have in your life and what lifestyle you want to actually fund. This will give you a better context to reference your financial aims against.

Check out the Coaching Business Blueprint (www.moreclientsmorecash.com/businessblueprint.html) to find out more about finding your compelling reasons for setting you your own business.

HOW TO GET COACHING CLIENTS

Question: *Surely by niching I am going alienate lots of potential customers but not throwing out a big enough net?*

My Comments: Niching is one of the big paradoxes in business. So many people are afraid to just aim at a narrow market as they feel they will miss out on more business. This is a complete myth and you must avoid this mindset. The more specific you can be when identifying your customer, so you can send messages that makes you sound as if you are talking to them personally, the more clients you will get.

As you read earlier in this book, think about selling a pair of socks. What do you say, how do you pitch this? Just think about that for a second.

Now how about if I asked you to sell a pair of pink fluffy socks to an eight year old girl?

HOW TO GET COACHING CLIENTS

If you flip this over so you are thinking as one of your customers, and you were an eight year old girl, the message about pink fluffy socks would resonate with you more than a message just about socks. Remember you cannot please everybody all of the time, you can please some people a lot of the time though.

Check out the Coaching Business Blueprint (www.moreclientsmorecash.com/business-blueprint.html) to find out more about finding your own niche so you aim all your marketing ideas towards this market.

Question: *I am a master practioner in NLP and have a distinction diploma in Advanced Coaching from a recognised Coaching School, what more prove do people want that I know my stuff?*

<u>My Comments</u>: Let's clear this one up, no one gives a dam about how many letters you have after you

name, and no one cares about what qualifications you have got. You must change your mindset and accept that at the moment people think "I don't know you and I don't like you".

You must build a relationship first and let people get to know you and so you gain their trust as an expert in your field. Then and only then will people be more interested in how you got to where you are today.

I cannot express how important it is to build relationships in today's business world. Slam selling for a quick buck will not give you a consistent steady stream of new clients.

Check out the Coaching Business Blueprint (www.moreclientsmorecash.com/business-blueprint.html) to find out more about building a relationship with prospective clients so you earn the right to sell to them.

HOW TO GET COACHING CLIENTS

Question: *I know coaching is fantastic and will help people so why won't people hire me?*

My Comments: You need to step away from the word coaching. There are too many coaches out there today with 80% of them being incongruent. I remember sitting at a breakfast meeting with this guy who was stuffing his face with sausages and his shirt ready to burst open as he was so overweight. He then stood up and said he can help people lose weight. Now this maybe true, he might know how to help people lose weight but the image he gave off hardly established him as the expert.

Now that is an extreme example where there is very visible evidence of incongruencey. You need to make sure you have enough options for your customers to get to know you and see what your fantastic coaching skills can do for them. You need to have a nice funnel of free tips that help your prospects feel some pain relief by following your advice, they need low cost options so they can feel safe spending money with you and learn what great value they get from you. Once the trust is there and the recognition of the value you offer is seen, then and only then people will spend money on your high end products and services.

Check out the Coaching Business Blueprint (www.moreclientsmorecash.com/business-blueprint.html) to find out more about putting together a strategy that will bring cash into your business.

Question: *I'm not technically minded so have spent thousands on getting Web Developers in, yet my site hasn't made a penny, what is wrong?*

<u>**My Comments**</u>: Ok time to be blunt here, if you are paying someone money to do your website for you, fire them immediately.

They maybe brilliant designers but they are not likely to be marketers.

HOW TO GET COACHING CLIENTS

Your website is you key tool to building a huge database of people interested in working with you. Your website is not there for you to massage your own ego, it is there to let people know they are in the right place for what is bothering them.

Anyone who arrives at your webpage must be in no doubt they are in the right place. Your page must be screaming out at them that you have the solution to their problems, so much so they will give you contact details in exchange it.

You can get web pages for free, you don't need to be spending thousands at this point when you are just testing your market for what it is looking for and is willing to spend money on.

So many people get what they think is a good idea, project it to the world then hang on to it with emotional attachment whilst it fails miserably.

HOW TO GET COACHING CLIENTS

If you can get into the testing mindset first, find what works then project it to the world you will have a very successful business. Check out the Coaching Business Blueprint (www.moreclientsmorecash.com/business-blueprint.html) to find out more about discovering a process that works for your market.

Question: *I have been going to Networking meetings for ages yet am not getting any business, what am I doing wrong?*

<u>**My Comments**</u>: There are some simple rules you must follow when generating leads for your business.

Firstly you should never go in looking for the quick sale. People do not like that type of sales behavior these days and also, it is near impossible to sell high end coaching packages straight off the bat. You need to let people get to know you so they know you are what they are looking for before they have spend any money.

The other issue here is putting all your eggs in one basket. Your marketing activities should cover more than one area. Each stream should be set up on its own merit and tested and measured until giving you the result you are looking for.

The point of all your marketing is to make people aware of you big fat bribe you are offering in order to exchange contact details. Your marketing should never be for a quick sale. You want to build the relationship and let the leads filter down the funnel.

By implementing this strategy, your time spent networking will allow you to find people who are either interesting in what you offer or help your group understand what you offer so they can point people in your direction. Never ever sell to a room when Networking, its all about building relationships and trust.

HOW TO GET COACHING CLIENTS

Check out the Coaching Business Blueprint (www.moreclientsmorecash.com/business-blueprint.html) to find out more about implementing marketing activities that deliver a stream of leads to your business.

Question: *I cannot afford a coach right now as I don't have enough cash in my business.*

My Comments: This is where you need ask yourself what you are actually trying to achieve. I cannot believe how many coaches resist having their own coach yet expect people to buy from them.

Its ok, I am as guilty as anyone of doing this but what I can tell you is, that the moment I embraced coaching as part of my business strategy, I started making money.

If you are NLP person, you should know full well that modeling success is a key tool. So if you are wondering why your business is failing, look at people who have succeed and model what they do!

If you don't think you can afford coaching, then get creative. What books can you read? What CD's can you listen to? Who can you learn from? Who can you offer you services in exchange with to get help?

Check out the Coaching Business Blueprint (www.moreclientsmorecash.com/business-blueprint.html) as this is where I modeled successful coaches and turned it into a simple to follow blueprint to show you the root to success in your chosen niche!

Printed in Great Britain by
Amazon.co.uk, Ltd.,
Marston Gate.